ADAPTATION and BIODIVERSITY

by Richard Worth

What roles do adaptation and biodiversity play in maintaining life on our planet?

Table of CONTENTS

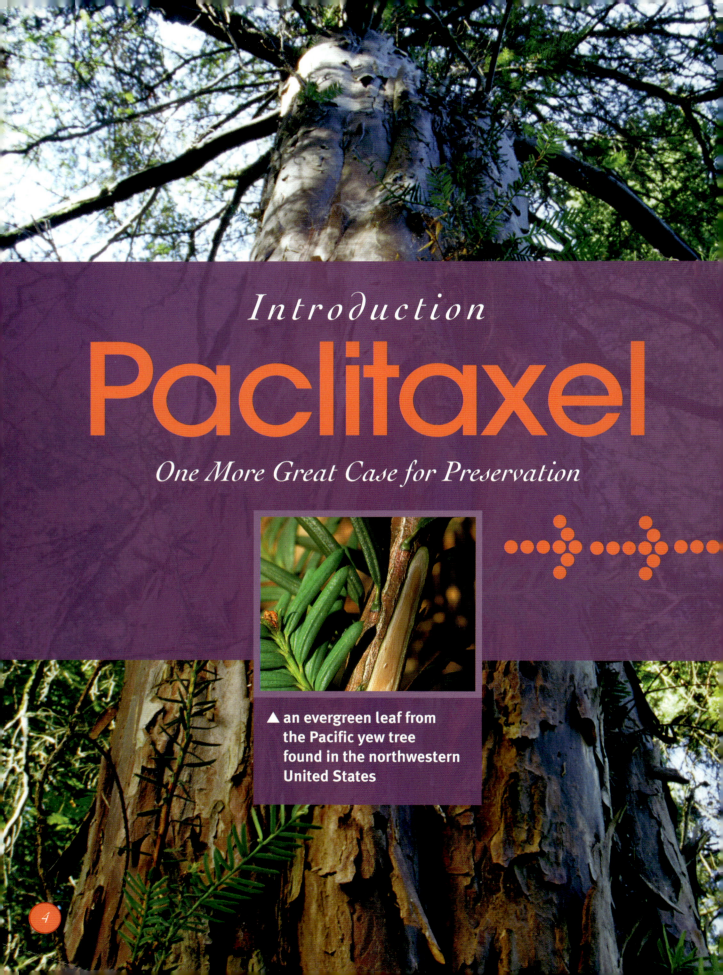

Introduction

Paclitaxel

One More Great Case for Preservation

▲ an evergreen leaf from the Pacific yew tree found in the northwestern United States

Paclitaxel is a cancer drug that originally came from a natural source—the Pacific yew tree found in the northwestern United States. The yew is well-adapted to grow in the rainy conditions of the Pacific Northwest. The yew is an evergreen with brown bark and an example of the rich biodiversity found in many forests. Paclitaxel comes from a fungus that lives in the bark of the tree and from the tree's needles. Removing the bark destroys the tree, so scientists have figured out how to produce a synthetic version of paclitaxel in the laboratory that is sold as a cancer treatment drug used in chemotherapy.

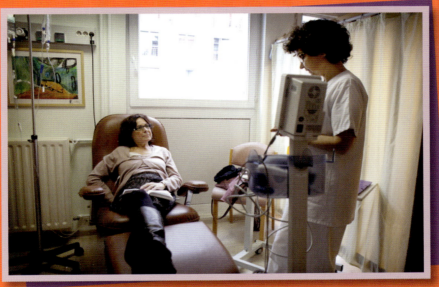

▲ woman receiving cancer treatment

Rain forests and other natural habitats around the world are being destroyed at an alarming rate and, as a result, many species of flora and fauna are becoming extinct. If the yew tree had become extinct, paclitaxel would never have been discovered. Millions of women have been treated successfully for breast and ovarian cancer with the drug, and without the yew tree, many of those lives would have been lost. This is just one example of how biodiversity—the variety of life forms that thrive on the planet—supports the survival of our species, the human animal.

Adaptation to Earth's HABITATS

The polar bear's heavy fur helps it adapt to the frigid conditions of the Arctic.

How have animals become adapted to survive in their habitats?

Perhaps you have spent part of a day walking in a park in early summer. You may have seen small birds, like sparrows, walking along the ground eating seeds. Possibly you heard a woodpecker hammering into a nearby tree, its sharp beak and long tongue perfectly adapted for finding insects inside the tree. Up above, a squirrel may be perched on a branch, eating an acorn. The trees themselves receive sunlight and rainwater that help them grow and flourish. The grass also stays green, like the trees, from frequent rain and abundant sunshine. In short, all of these living things are uniquely suited, or adapted, to their surroundings. **Adaptation** refers to a characteristic of an organism that increases its ability to survive in its environment.

Earth's Major Habitats

An animal or plant's **habitat** is the type of environment in which it can survive. The habitats on Earth fall into two broad categories—land and water— also referred to as **terrestrial** or **aquatic** habitats.

Terrestrial Habitats

One type of terrestrial habitat is temperate woodland, similar to the park with its trees and animals. The weather grows warm in summer, but usually not too warm. In autumn, many trees drop their leaves as the temperatures fall. Squirrels and chipmunks gather acorns and bury them to provide stores of food for winter.

Many birds fly southward in the autumn months; as their summer habitats change and grow colder, their sources of food disappear. Many of the birds that we see in the temperate zone today have either become adapted to the colder winter weather or have evolved migratory patterns that have taken them to warmer southern climates. Birds that fly south include yellow, black, and white warblers that rely on insects for food. The insects they prey upon die in the cold weather. As a result, those warblers that evolved a migratory pattern to Mexico and South America, where they could find plenty of insects, survived. Most, if not all, of those warblers that did not would have died off during the winter. If any survived, it may have been because they had a special characteristic, or adaptation, that enabled them to withstand the colder temperatures.

▲ Yellow warblers have become adapted to changing seasons by flying southward.

The Root of the Meaning
Terrestrial, Aquatic

Terrestrial comes from the Latin word *terra*, meaning "earth." **Aquatic** comes from the Latin word *aqua*, meaning "water."

Some animals, such as the groundhog, hibernate during the winter months. In **hibernation**, they spend the winter at rest. Before they hibernate, they eat plenty of food to produce a large layer of fat to live on during the winter. Then they go underground. Their heart rate goes from about 100 beats per minute to just about 4 beats per minute, breathing slows to one breath every 6 minutes, and their body temperature falls from about 32 degrees Celsius (90 degrees Fahrenheit) to about 4 degrees Celsius (39 degrees Fahrenheit), which is just above freezing. As a result, they need far less energy to survive. All these changes are examples of adaptations that enable the groundhog to survive harsh winters with little or no food supply. Groundhogs often remain in hibernation until the weather begins to grow warmer as spring approaches.

Some habitats are more extreme than the temperate environments. These include the Arctic region at the North Pole and the Antarctic region at the South Pole. The Arctic region is made up of the Arctic Ocean, a large number of islands, and northern areas of Canada, Asia, and Europe. Winters are long, with very little sunlight and the temperatures dipping to −30 degrees Celsius (−22 degrees Fahrenheit). Animals that live in the Arctic have adaptations that enable them to survive the cold winters.

For example, the arctic fox has a heavy coat of fur, and fur on its paws, to help keep it warm in cold, snowy winters. As snow begins to fall, the color of the fox's coat turns from gray to white. This camouflage not only helps the fox blend into the Arctic environment and avoid detection by larger animals that might prey on it, but also allows it to sneak up on its own prey undetected. The ptarmigan is a bird that also has camouflage to help it survive. It has a heavy coat of feathers that turns from brown to white in the snowy winters.

The Antarctic is a cold, arid continent where temperatures reach as low as −89 degrees Celsius (−128 degrees Fahrenheit)—the lowest temperatures naturally occurring on Earth's surface. Few animals live in this polar desert; however, a couple of **species**, or types, of penguins, and a few species of seals do live along the edges of the Antarctic continent. These animals usually stay close to the coast, spending time at the water looking for food. Penguins, for example, are flightless birds that have evolved flippers that propel them through the water in search of fish for food.

The groundhog hibernates during the winter. ▼

Text Structure
The phrase "as a result" signals a cause-and-effect relationship.

▲ Penguins have heavy layers of fat and flippers, adaptations to cold Antarctic waters.

▲ Kangaroo rats obtain the water they need from seeds.

Unlike Antarctica, most other deserts are hot. Examples include the Sahara Desert in Africa and the deserts in the southwestern United States. If you have lived, even for a short time, in New Mexico or Arizona, you have experienced a desert habitat. Temperatures can reach over 38 degrees Celsius (100 degrees Fahrenheit) during the day and become quite cold at night. The reason for these extreme temperature changes is that the desert holds very little moisture. It is this lack of moisture that results in the inability to retain heat after the sun has set and is the reason that there is a considerable drop in temperature at night.

Animals and plants that live in the desert have evolved important adaptations to enable them to survive the dry conditions. In deserts, rainfall averages only about 25 centimeters (10 inches) per year. Generally, cactus plants have a very extensive system of shallow roots. This allows them to quickly absorb as much water as possible before any moisture is evaporated in the hot, dry air. In addition, they can store water in their green stems. One of the most interesting adaptations is the way the leaves have evolved into the sharp, pointy, needle-like spines of the cactus, allowing the cactus to reduce water loss through transpiration and evaporation and also prevent animals from chewing on the water-rich stems. These adaptations help them survive during long dry periods.

Kangaroo rats require little or no rainfall to survive. They eat tiny seeds that contain enough water for the rats to live. During the day, kangaroo rats stay inside their holes to avoid the hot desert sun. At night, they venture out into the desert when temperatures are cooler.

The desert environment supports a rich **biodiversity** of living organisms. There are a great variety of plants and animals adapted to live in the harsh desert conditions.

SCIENCE & MATH

Use these formulas to convert Fahrenheit (F) to Celsius (C) and vice versa.

$$F = 9/5 \; C + 32 \qquad C = 5/9 \; (F - 32)$$

Aquatic Habitats

Aquatic habitats differ from each other by the amount of salt in the water, or **salinity**. Oceans, for example, are considered saltwater bodies that by definition have a much greater salinity than freshwater rivers and lakes. At the mouth of a river, where it runs into the sea, there is a mixture of fresh water and salt water called an estuary.

▲ The ocean is a type of aquatic habitat.

The oceans are inhabited by numerous types of organisms and are therefore rich in biodiversity. Aquatic life-forms range from mammoth whales to microscopic floating organisms called **zooplankton**. These zooplankton are eaten by fish, which are eaten by larger fish, which in turn become prey for even larger organisms like dolphins and whales.

Among the most important animals found in oceans are coral. Coral are small animals with soft bodies and tentacles that are used for catching even smaller organisms. As coral reproduce, the new organisms remain connected to the older coral. Among the types of food that coral eat are small bacteria found in the sea. They provide nutrients that help coral produce hard skeletons. When the coral dies, its skeleton is added to those of previous generations. After many, many generations, large coral reefs are formed.

Coral reefs thrive in clear, shallow water that remains above 20 degrees Celsius (68 degrees Fahrenheit). Within these reefs live many other types of ocean plants and animals. However, the reefs can be destroyed if the clear ocean water becomes polluted by farms or manufacturing plants near shore. When the coral die, the reefs stop growing and eventually are destroyed by environmental conditions.

▲ Coral reefs can thrive only in clear, shallow, warm water.

Some aquatic environments, such as ponds, lakes, streams, and rivers, contain fresh water. North America has a number of large rivers, such as the Hudson, Ohio, Mississippi, Missouri, and Colorado. Like other freshwater habitats around the world, these rivers provide homes to a diverse range of plants and animals.

▲ The United States has large rivers in the eastern, central, and western states. In addition to hosting countless species, these rivers are used to irrigate farm lands, to transport goods, and for recreation.

Along shorelines, for example, are long-legged birds called egrets and herons. They stand in the shallow waters and wait for fish to appear. As a fish swims by, the heron pokes its long bill—especially adapted for its task of spearing fish—into the water to catch its prey.

Other birds, such as ducks and swans, spend much of their time floating in deeper waters of lakes and ponds. These birds rely on freshwater plants for a large part of their diets. Other animals, such as muskrats, might be seen swimming in rivers and ponds. Muskrats build their homes in burrows along the riverbanks with an entrance hidden below the water.

◀ Muskrats eat freshwater plants and smaller animals.

Among the most common types of animals found in freshwater habitats are frogs. These **amphibians**—animals that can live in water and on land—eat worms and capture insects with long, sticky tongues. Frogs receive part of the oxygen they need to survive through the water in their habitats. Frogs obtain oxygen by forcing air from the atmosphere into their lungs. This air then diffuses from the lungs into their circulatory system and travels to their cells. Frogs can also obtain oxygen by diffusion across their moist, thin skin. Since frogs spend much of their time in the water, those that had the ability to obtain oxygen by this second method had a greater chance of survival than those that had thicker skin and/or fewer blood vessels beneath the skin. Adaptations, such as thin skin and abundant blood vessels beneath the skin, increase the frog's chances of survival. We can describe the frog as being adapted to a watery environment. If, during the summer, there's a particularly hot period and a pond begins to dry up, frogs can bury themselves in the mud to keep cool and to keep their skin moist. While they're buried, they enter a period of dormancy, called **estivation**, during which their heart rate and breathing slow down. This is similar to the changes they undergo during hibernation, which occurs in the winter.

Adaptation to Changing Habitats

Over time, habitats may change and affect the plants and animals living there. For example, a wooded area may be cleared to provide building lots for homes. Birds that migrated to the woodland each spring may no longer have a place to nest and find food. Some birds, in the migrating population, may find a similar habitat close to the original one and be able to nest there. Other members of the population may be able to move into a slightly different habitat if they happen to have some characteristics that enable them to survive in the new environment. We could say that the birds were preadapted to this environment. If birds can't find a similar habitat or a new habitat to which they are at least minimally adapted, they will die off.

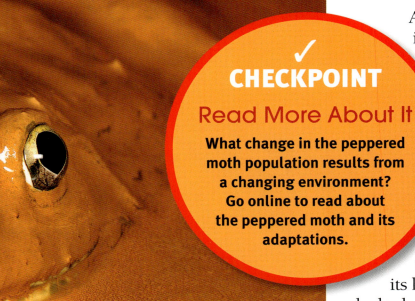

✓
CHECKPOINT

Read More About It

What change in the peppered moth population results from a changing environment? Go online to read about the peppered moth and its adaptations.

▲ **A frog adapts to hot, dry summers through estivation, burying itself in mud and slowing its heart and breathing rates.**

Other environmental changes may affect much more than a small wooded area and the local populations that live in that limited area. For example, because the polar caps continue to melt, a much larger geographic area will be altered and all of the populations of species living in that area will be affected. If we use the Arctic Circle as an example, it may be possible that polar bears will find that there is no place for them to live and all of them will die off. If this were to happen, we would say that the polar bear species has become **extinct**, or died out.

Another example, closer to home, is a species called the ivory-billed woodpecker, which hasn't been seen in years and may already be extinct. This large woodpecker is about 51 centimeters (20 inches) in length. Its habitat was large swamps and pine forests in the American South. The woodpecker lived on insects, especially those found in dead trees. With its long bill, the bird pecked at the bark, tearing it away, and eating the insects behind it. Each male and female pair of ivory-billed woodpeckers relied on an area of 26 square kilometers (about 10 square miles) to find enough food to survive and feed their young.

However, during the last half of the nineteenth century, logging companies destroyed thousands of woodland acres. They cut down the trees for building and other purposes. The ivory-billed woodpeckers could not adapt to a changing environment and disappeared.

▼ **The ivory-billed woodpecker could not adapt to a changing environment and may be extinct.**

Hands-On Science
An Animal's Preferred Habitat

TIME: Approximately 2 days

MATERIALS:
- A medium-size cardboard box with a top
- A spray bottle filled with water
- 2 small bags of peat moss
- 1 box of oatmeal
- 1 small pail of sand
- 1 small pail of leaves
- 3 earthworms
- 1 pair of scissors

Step 1: With scissors, cut the lid of the box in half (across its width).

Step 2: Place the peat moss in one half of the box and put some oatmeal on top of the peat moss.

Step 3: Place sand and leaves in the other half of the box.

Step 4: Cut small holes in one of the halves of the lid and place that half on the side of the box with the peat moss and oatmeal.

Step 5: Cut a small door in the other half of the lid and place this half between the peat moss/oatmeal and the sand/leaves.

Step 6: Dig up 3 worms and place them in the open side of the box.

Step 7: Place the box in an area that gets some sunlight and keep the covered side moist with the spray bottle.

Step 8: Record your observations. What changes, if any, do you observe after 2 days? What explanations might you give to explain these observations?

Summing Up

- Earth contains two broad types of habitats. These are terrestrial habitats and aquatic habitats.

- Terrestrial habitats differ by the range of temperature in them and the amount of precipitation that they receive.

- Most aquatic habitats are freshwater or saltwater, but a few are a mixture of both.

- Organisms that have become adapted to their habitats survive. Organisms that have not become adapted either seek other habitats, evolve characteristics that adapt them to different habitats, or become extinct.

Putting It All Together

Choose one of the following research activities. Work independently, in pairs, or in small groups. Share your responses with your class.

1. Make a list of the animals that live in your neighborhood during spring or summer. How has each adapted to the habitat?

2. Research an animal, such as the dodo, that has become extinct. Why did the extinction occur?

3. River deltas contain a combination of fresh water and salt water. Research the types of plants adapted to conditions in the Mississippi River delta and prepare a visual presentation on this ecosystem.

EVOLUTION of Life

What is Charles Darwin's theory of evolution?

Much of the information that we have about adaptation and biodiversity comes from the work of Charles Darwin, a nineteenth-century scientist. Darwin was born in Shrewsbury, England, in 1809. His father was a doctor who hoped that Charles would follow in his footsteps. In fact, Charles worked closely with his father as he treated his patients. In 1825, he was sent to the University of Edinburgh Medical School in Scotland to become a doctor.

Charles had very little interest in his medical studies. Instead, he joined a group of other students who were interested in studying nature. Indeed, Darwin did so poorly at Edinburgh that in 1828 his father finally sent him to Cambridge University in England to study for the priesthood. Nevertheless, Charles continued his studies of natural history. He collected beetles and wrote some of his observations, which were published in a magazine. At Cambridge, Darwin studied with a well-known science professor named John Stevens Henslow.

Darwin showed an interest ▼ in natural history when he was still a young man.

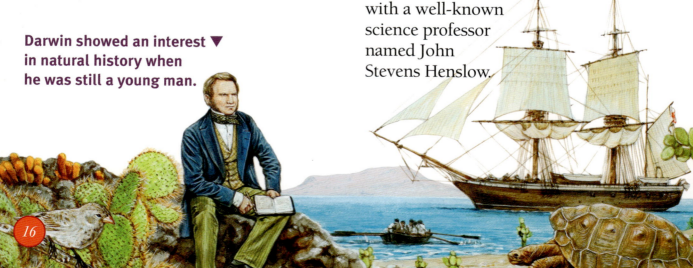

Professor Henslow knew that a sailing ship named the HMS *Beagle* was making a voyage to South America. The purpose of the voyage was to study the geography of the area as well as the animals and plants that lived there. The captain of the *Beagle*, Robert FitzRoy, was looking for a young naturalist to accompany the expedition. Professor Henslow recommended Darwin.

The HMS *Beagle* left England on a five-year voyage at the end of December in 1831. It sailed down the west coast of Africa, stopping at the Cape Verde Islands. There, Darwin went ashore to explore the geography of the area. High up in the mountains he discovered fossils of sea shells. These **fossils** were the remains of dead sea animals. At one time they had lived in the water, but the shore must have risen at some much earlier date to form the mountains. This theory had been proposed by a scientist named Charles Lyell. Darwin had been reading Lyell's book, *Principles of Geology*, on his voyage. Lyell observed that forces such as earthquakes and volcanic eruptions had changed the surface of Earth throughout history. Lyell also wrote that these forces continued to act in the present.

✓
CHECKPOINT
Visualize It

Read some of the field studies and descriptions in Darwin's observation log and visualize the animals and plants he saw on his journey.

▲ Darwin's observations of the Galápagos tortoises helped him develop his theories of evolution.

17

From the coast of Africa, the HMS *Beagle* sailed for South America. There Darwin found more evidence to support Lyell's theories. He discovered fossils of sea shells in high cliffs along with the fossils of enormous animals that had become extinct. The *Beagle* rounded the tip of South America and sailed northward, eventually reaching the Galápagos Islands, off the coast of Ecuador. The islands are named after the giant Galápagos tortoise.

Darwin noticed that the tortoises were not the same on every island. Some tortoises were larger than others, with domed shells and short necks. On other islands, the necks were longer and the shells were shaped differently. The

◀ **The HMS *Beagle* was a survey ship that collected information about various locations around the world.**

climate was also different from island to island, and Darwin later began to wonder if tortoises had somehow adapted to these conditions, ". . . to adapt and alter the race to [a] changing world," as he wrote in one of his notebooks.

The HMS *Beagle* left the Galápagos Islands, sailed through the Pacific Ocean, rounded the tip of Africa, and arrived in England in October 1836. By the time he returned home, Darwin was already well known. He had written letters containing his observations, and some of them had already been published.

SCIENCE & HISTORY

Lamarck's Theories

Approximately sixty years before Darwin published his theory of evolution, Jean-Baptiste Lamarck, a French scientist, published his thoughts on the subject. The two major ideas in Lamarck's theory were:

1. Organisms could acquire new characteristics through the use of structures that they already had or lose specific structures because they didn't use them.

2. Those structures acquired through use or lost through disuse could be inherited by their offspring. Lamarck believed that an animal's environment leads to adaptations and changes in the animal over time. For example, moles lost most of their eyesight because they live underground and do not need to see.

▲ **The different-shaped beaks of the finches that Darwin collected helped him understand the development of different species.**

EVERYDAY SCIENCE

Breeding a Dachshund

Dachshunds are unusually shaped dogs. They are long, with short legs, and have often been called wiener dogs because they resemble hot dogs. They were bred in Germany several hundred years ago to hunt badgers. In fact, the name *dachshund* in German means "badger dog." Through selective breeding, German dog owners developed hounds with short legs and long bodies. This new breed of dog was perfectly suited for going down into holes and flushing out badgers so hunters could kill them. The badgers attacked horses and other animals. Smaller dachshunds, miniatures, were bred to go into rabbit holes and chase out rabbits so they could be killed for food.

Dachshunds were bred to chase badgers and rabbits. ▶

After his return, Darwin began an intense study of his observations and the thousands of animal species he had collected during his voyage. Among these species were a variety of small birds called finches. Each had a different-shaped beak. Later, Darwin theorized that all of them had somehow developed, or evolved, from a single species of finch. But over thousands of years, they had developed different-shaped beaks, each one an adaptation to their environment that enabled them to eat the food they found there.

To formulate some of his theories of adaptation and **evolution**, Darwin drew upon the work of an English economist named Thomas Malthus. According to Malthus, human populations were too large for all of them to survive. As a result, some people starved because there was not enough food. Others died from disease and never reached adulthood. Darwin realized that the same thing happened among animals and plants. More animals and plants were produced than could survive. The traits of those that did survive would be passed on, from generation to generation, for thousands of years. "The result of this," he wrote, "would be the formation of new species," such as the various types of finches or Galápagos tortoises. It's important to realize that Darwin did not know how these traits were passed from one generation to the next. In fact, he tried to explain this by using Lamarck's incorrect idea of the inheritance of acquired characteristics. With time, as the science of genetics was developed, scientists had a better understanding of how traits were inherited.

Darwin Develops His Theory of Evolution

Darwin's Theory of Evolution

Darwin's theory of evolution is based upon the concepts of:

1. variation (no two organisms are identical)

2. overproduction (more organisms are born than can survive)

3. struggle for existence (competition among members of a population)

4. natural selection (the environment determines the better-adapted organism)

In *On the Origin of Species,* Charles Darwin set down the principles of evolution. ▶

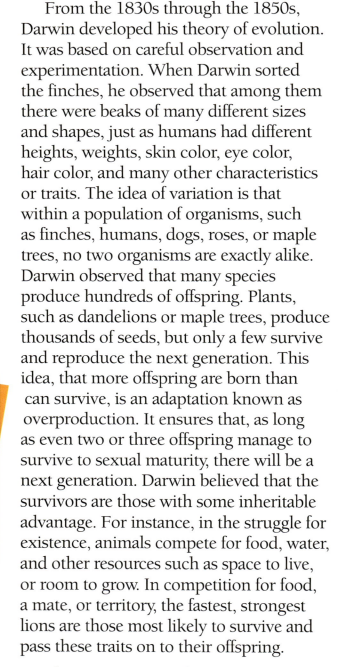

From the 1830s through the 1850s, Darwin developed his theory of evolution. It was based on careful observation and experimentation. When Darwin sorted the finches, he observed that among them there were beaks of many different sizes and shapes, just as humans had different heights, weights, skin color, eye color, hair color, and many other characteristics or traits. The idea of variation is that within a population of organisms, such as finches, humans, dogs, roses, or maple trees, no two organisms are exactly alike. Darwin observed that many species produce hundreds of offspring. Plants, such as dandelions or maple trees, produce thousands of seeds, but only a few survive and reproduce the next generation. This idea, that more offspring are born than can survive, is an adaptation known as overproduction. It ensures that, as long as even two or three offspring manage to survive to sexual maturity, there will be a next generation. Darwin believed that the survivors are those with some inheritable advantage. For instance, in the struggle for existence, animals compete for food, water, and other resources such as space to live, or room to grow. In competition for food, a mate, or territory, the fastest, strongest lions are those most likely to survive and pass these traits on to their offspring.

The environment determines which flower will be pollinated, or which animal will catch its prey. If

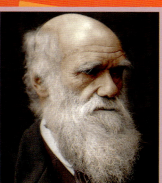

◀ **Frogs produce many eggs that turn into tadpoles, but only a few survive.**

Parents pass on their traits to their offspring.

one flower has a color or odor that attracts a pollinator, it may have a better chance than another flower of producing seeds and, therefore, the next generation. If one predator is faster or able to make quicker, sharper turns than another, it may catch its dinner and survive to find a mate and reproduce. But change the environment and the variation that made one flower or one predator better adapted than another may no longer be an adaptation. There may be an entirely different outcome. This is why Darwin's theory is called **natural selection**. Nature, the environment, does the selecting or determination of which variation serves as an adaptation. Darwin also studied **selective breeding**. In selective breeding, breeders try to select specific traits in animals or plants to be reproduced in the next generations. Instead of natural selection, this is artificial selection. For instance, several dogs of a single species might have litters of six puppies. One of those puppies in each litter has a slight variation from the rest—shorter legs, longer hair, or a different color coat. The breeder wants to produce more dogs with these traits and so breeds the two dogs with these variations, eventually creating a new species.

Darwin based his theory of evolution on a variety of data. From the work of scientists like Lyell, Darwin concluded that life on Earth had a long history. He could also see from his own observations of fossils that the origins of life on Earth stretched far back through time. From his observations of plants and animals, Darwin realized that they produce many offspring. Turtles lay many eggs. But only some of these eggs survive. Frogs give birth to hundreds of offspring. Some are eaten by predators, others die from disease, and still others die because of lack of food. If they all survived, the world would be overrun by a particular species.

From observing animals and plants, Darwin knew traits are passed on through a species' offspring. When two finches mate, they produce tiny finches with the same traits as their parents. They don't give birth to robins or red-headed woodpeckers. But each of these tiny finches, although they look very much alike, may have a few traits that are different from those of the others. Perhaps one of these has a slight difference in coloring or a beak that is slightly different. All of these finches do not survive. But those with a certain variation may survive because their trait—their beak or their coloring—may adapt them for survival.

Darwin conducted many experiments with barnacles, the tiny sea organisms that attach themselves to rocks and the bottoms of ships. Over eight years of study, Darwin demonstrated that some of these organisms changed—that is, they evolved—as their environment changed. These adaptations helped them survive, and they won the struggle for survival over their competitors. As the fittest to survive, they passed on their traits to the next generation.

In 1859, Darwin published his findings in a book called *On the Origin of Species*. Only 1,250 copies of the book were published, but all of them were sold within a single day. This book changed the way that many people thought about the development of life on Earth. In the introduction to the book, Darwin wrote:

"As many more individuals of each species are born than can possibly survive; and as, consequently, there is a frequently recurring struggle for existence, it follows that any being, if it vary however slightly in any manner profitable to itself, under the complex and sometimes varying conditions of life, will have a better chance of surviving, and thus be naturally selected. From this strong principle of inheritance, any selected variety will tend to [reproduce] its new and modified form."

SCIENCE & LITERATURE

Coauthors of Theory

Alfred Wallace, like Charles Darwin, was a British naturalist. But unlike Darwin, Wallace came from a poor family, and circumstances forced him to leave school at age thirteen. However, this did not keep him from reading and learning on his own. In fact, he read many of the same books that Darwin had read, such as Malthus's *An Essay on the Principle of Population*, and even a published account of Darwin's adventures on the HMS *Beagle*. Also like Darwin, Wallace was a great collector of specimens, took extensive notes, and communicated his ideas through letter writing. One of those letters was written to Darwin in June 1858. After reading it, Darwin was shocked to see that Wallace had come to the same conclusions as he had and used almost the exact same language.

This sent Darwin into a panic because he had hesitated over putting all of his thoughts about evolution into a book and having it published. Darwin didn't want to lose all the credit for his work, but at the same time, he wanted to give Wallace credit for his discoveries. After discussing the issue with friends and scientists, Wallace's letter and enclosed manuscript and an earlier draft of Darwin's theory, which predated Wallace's, were presented simultaneously to the Linnean Society, and both shared credit for their theory of evolution through the process of natural selection.

Summing Up

- During the nineteenth century, a scientist named Charles Darwin revolutionized the way that people thought about life on Earth.

- From his travels, experiments, and observations, Darwin proposed a theory of evolution.

- Darwin's theory accounted for the way that species develop, adapt, and survive in their environments.

Putting It All Together

Choose one of the following research activities. Work independently, in pairs, or in small groups. Share your responses with your class.

1. Research the Galápagos Islands. Choose one indigenous plant or animal species from the Galápagos and write a short illustrated report on how it has become adapted to its home.

2. Using your school library and the Internet, do further research into the life of Alfred Wallace. Prepare a short presentation on Wallace's work.

3. Darwin's theories were widely criticized and feared when they were published. Read about the reactions to Darwin's theories and prepare arguments for and against his theories.

BIODIVERSITY:
Development of a
Species

How has life developed and changed on Earth?

◀ **The lobe-finned fish evolved into amphibians.**

Scientists estimate that Earth is approximately 4.5 billion years old. The first life forms began to appear about 3.9 billion years ago during the Archean eon. These life forms were tiny organisms called bacteria that were made up of only a single cell. During the Archean eon, tiny, blue-green algae, similar to plants, also made their appearance. These algae had the ability to absorb carbon dioxide from the air and combine it with sunlight to produce sugar and oxygen. They used the sugar to nourish themselves. The sugar in algae would also provide a source of food for other organisms. Increasing amounts of oxygen produced by the algae would enable other forms of life to thrive.

Cambrian Period

From these early forms of life, multicelled life forms evolved. Approximately 540 million years ago, during the Cambrian period, trilobites appeared in the ocean waters. **Trilobites** were multicelled organisms with three different sections and hard shells. There are many fossil remains of the trilobites, which populated the seas for 300 million years before a mass extinction occurred, killing off many animal species, including the trilobites.

Over the next 70 million years, other forms of life emerged, including coral, fish, and plants similar to ferns, which became the first plants to grow on land. Fish had also been evolving into a class of lobe-finned organisms that had well-developed bones with attached muscles. Fish with these strong, fleshy fins were able to support themselves on land and perhaps even walk in some rudimentary way. Equally remarkable is that some of the lobe-finned fish developed lungs, making it possible for certain species to support their body above the water's surface while in shallow areas and gulp at air. At one time, it was believed that four-legged land animals evolved from a species of air-gulping fish with lungs. Today most scientists believe that they evolved independently.

Trilobites were a major life-form in the Cambrian period. ▼

SCIENCE AND MATH

How long is an eon? An eon ranges in length from nearly 600 million years to nearly 2 billion years. There are four eons in geologic time:

PRE-ARCHEAN EON
(or Hadean eon) 4.6 billion to 3.8 billion years ago—Scientists believe the moon and Earth were created during this eon.

ARCHEAN EON
3.8 billion to 2.5 billion years ago—Single-celled organisms and algae came into existence in this eon.

PROTEROZOIC EON
2.5 billion to 570 million years ago—Multicelled life appeared during this eon.

PHANEROZOIC EON
570 million years ago to the present—Complex life evolved during this time.

Permian Period

During the Permian period, from 300 million to 250 million years ago, amphibians and reptiles evolved into a large number of various species. A single species consists of those animals that have similar features and can reproduce with one another. Insects, which had begun to appear earlier, also became far more numerous. As more and more plants grew on land, the amount of oxygen increased, nourishing a much larger population of animals. Some were **herbivores**, or plant eaters. These herbivores, in turn, became prey for **carnivores**, or meat-eating animals.

Reptiles evolved from amphibians, and dinosaurs evolved from these ancestral reptiles. The earliest dinosaurs date back to the late Triassic period, about 228 million years ago. During the next two periods, the Jurassic and Cretaceous, dinosaurs gave rise to many different types and became the dominant life form

The Root of the Meaning
Niche

Niche comes from a French word *nicher*, meaning "to make a nest or a place."

on Earth. The Brachiosaurus was a large herbivore, while Tyrannosaurus rex was a massive carnivore. However, by the end of the Cretaceous period, 65 million years ago, all dinosaurs became extinct. Today the only living remnants of these mighty animals are birds. Living at the same time as the dinosaurs were other types of reptiles such as crocodiles and snakes, as well as mammals, birds, many types of insects, and other animals.

The extinction of the dinosaurs freed up the niches they had occupied. The reduced competition and this new ecological opportunity made possible a more rapid evolution and diversification of mammals. With time, mammals became the new dominant life form on the planet. Some of these mammals, which also have become extinct, were the giant sloths and the woolly mammoths, as well as smaller organisms, like cats and deer. These changes occurred in the geological era known as the Cenozoic, which has come to be called the "Age of Mammals." Late in the Cenozoic, some prehistoric or primitive mammal evolved into modern man.

◄ The woolly mammoth was a massive mammal that lived in cold regions.

Adaptation and Increase in Biodiversity

As animals adapt to their environment, they may evolve into different species. In the Galápagos, for example, Darwin saw different species of finches. Because of environmental (natural) selection pressures, an ancestral population of birds diverged into several related but slightly different birds.

This type of development is called divergent evolution. In **divergent evolution**, different species evolve from the same ancestor through the process of natural selection. Another example of divergent evolution is the various species of foxes. A kit fox can be found in the desert. It has a gray and rusty-colored coat that enables it to blend in with the environment and avoid detection by both its predators and its prey. To deal with the high temperatures of the desert, the kit fox developed larger ears. These give the fox more surface area to disperse heat and remain as cool as possible.

In contrast, the arctic fox has a white coat that enables it to blend in with the snow of the cold northern climate. In addition, the arctic fox has smaller ears, so less heat escapes, keeping it warmer in cold winters. A third type of fox, the red fox, lives in forests. Its color helps provide the red fox with camouflage to elude its predators. Because the kit fox and the red fox have many similar structures, it can be inferred that they are related through some common ancestor. However, as they became adapted to their different environments, they became more dissimilar, or further diverged from each other.

The whale and the bat are linked through divergent evolution. The wing of the bat and the fin of the whale have a similar shape. The bat's wings propel it through the air in pursuit of insects. The side fin of a whale helps propel it through the water in pursuit of fish. Both have similar shapes and similar bones as well as many different features that have adapted both animals for their environments. At some point, the two animals took divergent paths on the evolutionary road.

▼ **The kit fox, the arctic fox, and the red fox developed through divergent evolution.**

the kit fox

the arctic fox

the red fox

27

In **convergent evolution**, two unrelated species develop similar features to survive in a similar environment. An example is the duck-billed platypus and the mallard duck. Each has a similar bill because both animals find food by pushing their bills through mud and sifting out tiny organisms to eat. However, the duck is a bird and the platypus is a mammal. They have completely different ancestors.

Two different species of plants may have developed similar shapes to help them hold water in the dry deserts. The cactus can be found in the desert of the American Southwest. A similar plant, but completely unrelated to the cactus, is the euphorbia. It grows in the African deserts. These pairs of animals and plants fill a similar niche.

A **niche** is a plant or animal's place in the environment and what it must do to survive in that place. Think of it as a job—what people do to support themselves and to purchase food as well as other necessities. Electricians install lighting fixtures and other electrical devices in homes and offices. This is their niche, and they have skills that enable them to fill it successfully. By doing their work effectively, they can make money to support themselves and their families.

Extinctions

In some cases, an animal's niche changes. If it cannot adapt, then its population may decline and the species may even become extinct. Mass extinctions have occurred throughout geologic time. For example, a mass extinction occurred at the end of the Permian period that led to the disappearance of the trilobites. Scientists look at the fossil record in the rocks. In older layers, they find trilobites, but in newer layers after the end of the Permian period, there are no more trilobite fossils. A change in the environment caused by global cooling or numerous eruptions by volcanoes may have led to their extinction. Not only was it the trilobites that became extinct, but as many as nine out of ten of all living organisms were destroyed during the mass extinction.

✓ CHECKPOINT

Make Connections

Have you ever found or seen a fossil? What was it a fossil of, and where did you see it?

At the end of the Cretaceous period, the dinosaurs became extinct. ▶

Another mass extinction occurred 65 million years ago at the end of the Cretaceous period. This led to the extinction of the dinosaurs. Not only did the living dinosaurs die, but they ceased producing offspring. Dinosaurs were egg layers. Any young that hatched after the older dinosaurs had been killed were tiny, easy prey for the animals that had survived the mass extinction. Therefore, no young dinosaurs survived to take their place in the ecosystem, and no new species of dinosaur appeared to replace those that had died.

Scientists have developed several theories to account for the disappearance of the dinosaurs. According to one theory, an enormous asteroid, between 10 and 19 kilometers (6 and 12 miles) wide, crashed into Earth's surface, creating vast clouds of dust on impact that rose into the sky and prevented sunlight from reaching Earth's surface. Another theory is that it was ash and dust from a known increase in volcanic eruptions that blocked out the sun. Other scientists hypothesize that climate change drastically cooled Earth's surface. In each case, the lack of sunlight or the colder climate killed the vegetation that supported the dinosaurs' food chain, eventually forcing them, and presumably many other species, into extinction.

Horses began to appear about 55 million years ago. ▶

Rise of the Mammal

During the period that dinosaurs dominated Earth, **mammals**—animals with hair that nurse their young—also began to appear. The earliest mammals came on the scene about 90 to 200 million years ago and were probably small, similar to modern shrews, which may have enabled them to hide from the dinosaurs and survive.

These small mammals survived the mass extinction that killed off the dinosaurs. Mammals were much safer now and began to explore and take advantage of niches previously dominated by the dinosaurs.

▲ **Mammals similar in size to this modern shrew began to appear about 90 million years ago.**

About 10 million years after the mass extinction, fossil records show a large increase in the species of mammals. As Earth warmed during this period, plants probably increased, giving mammals more food to eat.

One of the herbivores that began its long development was the horse. It was the size of a dog about 55 million years ago, and like dogs, the early horse had toes on its front and back feet. Gradually, the climate in North America became drier, forests grew smaller, and grassy plains increased. Meanwhile, early horses had evolved specialized teeth, for eating tough grass, and longer legs, which gave them the ability to run across the plains, find food, and escape their predators. Various species of horses developed. Those with toes died out and those with single hoofs are the ancestors of *Equus*, the modern horse.

Appearing 4.5 million years ago, somewhat earlier than *Equus*, was another large mammal, the mammoth. Like the ancestors of *Equus*, mammoths became a very diversified group with a wide range of habitats. The best known of these was the woolly mammoth, which lived about 120,000 to 150,000 years ago. Relatives of the elephant, woolly mammoths had large, hairy bodies, giant tusks, small ears and weighed about 5 tons. Many of these traits served the huge herbivores well during a period when Earth became much colder. Then, as Earth's climate began to warm about 12,000 years ago, the glaciers decreased and forests began to expand into the grasslands, reducing the grazing lands needed by the woolly mammoth. Unable to adapt their eating habits to the changing conditions, they began to die off. Meanwhile, the warming climate enabled another species to expand its living areas: humans.

Rise of the Human

The evolution of humans probably began about 4.5 million years ago. Like the great apes, humans had adapted opposable thumbs, which allow the hands to grasp objects. The human's spine curvature, thigh bone, and feet all make it possible for them to walk upright. About 2.4 million years ago, modern man's earliest ancestor evolved into a species known as *Homo habilis*, nicknamed "handy man" because members of this species had learned to use stone tools to cut meat off dead animals in order to survive in its environment.

Approximately 1.8 million years ago, *Homo erectus* appeared, possibly evolving from *Homo habilis*. The human brain in this species had grown larger, almost to its size today. These humans had developed knowledge of fire, which they used to cook their food. They fashioned weapons to kill animals and made their own simple clothing so they could live in colder regions. *Homo sapiens*, modern humans, first made their appearance about 200,000 years ago. For many thousands of years, they lived side by side with another species, Neanderthals, who disappeared about 35,000 years ago.

Gradually, our ancestors built shelters to protect themselves from the harsh weather and developed tools and weapons to farm the land and hunt other species.

Summing Up

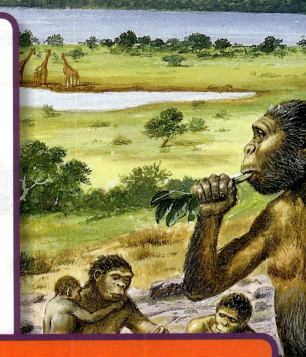

- Living organisms have developed across eons of geologic time.

- Successful species have occupied a niche in the environment that has enabled them to survive. Unsuccessful species have been unable to adapt to changing environments.

- Even highly successful organisms like the dinosaurs, which dominated Earth for millions of years, were unable to survive the mass extinctions that occurred 65 million years ago.

- As dinosaurs disappeared, other organisms took their place. These included small mammals and finally humans.

Putting It All Together

Choose one of the following research activities. Work independently, in pairs, or in small groups. Share your responses with your class.

1. Research the plants and animals that were alive during the dinosaur age. Create a diorama of this period.

2. Research some of the ways in which *Homo sapiens* adapted to their environment. Prepare a presentation for the class describing these adaptations.

3. Read about the evolution of the giraffe. Create drawings to show how the giraffe has changed over many thousands of years.

OH, TO THE CONTRARY, THEY DO NOT. THEY COULD NOT COMPETE FOR THE SAME RESOURCES AND SURVIVE IN THIS HABITAT IF THEY WERE ALL THE SAME! THUS THEY HAVE DIFFERENT WINGS AND PLUMAGE AND MORE THAN NINE DIFFERENT BEAK TYPES ALONE! THERE ARE BEAKS FOR TEARING, CRACKING, SIPPING, DRILLING, PICKING, PROBING, STRIKING, STRAINING, AND SCOOPING.

THERE ARE FEET FOR SWIMMING, HUNTING, WALKING, PERCHING, CLIMBING, AND WADING!

I THINK I'M ADAPTING AS WE SPEAK . . .

SO EACH SPECIES HAD TO DEVELOP ITS OWN NICHE, HAVING ADAPTED ITS BEAK AND FEET, WINGS, OR EVEN BIRDSONG OVER THE GENERATIONS FOR OPTIMUM SURVIVAL.

NOW THAT'S WORTH WADING FOR!

EXPLAIN WHY BIODIVERSITY IS CRUCIAL FOR SURVIVAL. WHAT ARE SOME WAYS HUMANS HAVE ADAPTED OVER TIME?

Chapter 4

Interactions Among
Living
THINGS

How do animals, plants, and humans interact?

Kudzu is a large-leafed vine of Japanese origin that became a popular addition to American gardens during the 1800s. Later, in the 1930s and 1940s, the vine was planted on farms to help prevent soil erosion and soon thrived in the South, where the warm climate enabled it to grow as much as 0.3 meter (1 foot) per day. Before long, kudzu had invaded many acres of land, crowding out other types of green plants and growing over other species of trees and bushes, preventing them from receiving sunlight. By the 1970s, the U.S. Department of Agriculture had labeled kudzu a weed and an invasive species.

The story of kudzu illustrates one type of interaction among living organisms known as competition. Competition exists among different species for the same niche in the environment.

Competition can also occur between organisms of the same species. Male red-winged blackbirds are known by the red patch on their wings. In the Northeast, the blackbirds stake out a territory or a tree during the spring where they find food and try to attract a mate. If a rival blackbird wants to take over the territory, he often tries to hide his red patch under his black feathers. In this way, his competition does not recognize him as another red-winged blackbird until it is too late. By that time, the rival can establish himself in the territory, drive out his competitor, and take over.

Another type of interaction among living organisms is called **mutualism**. In this case, different species depend on each other in a way that mutually benefits both of them. The relationship between flowers and various species of birds and insects provides a good example. Trumpet vines, with their long, showy flowers, attract hummingbirds. The trumpet flowers are perfectly designed for a hummingbird to hover outside, stick its long bill into the flower, and drink its nectar. Meanwhile, some of the pollen from the flower sticks to the bird, which carries it to another plant. As a result of this adaptation, the hummingbird is nourished and the trumpet vine ensures pollination. The plant can consequently produce seeds that will ensure the survival of new trumpet vines.

◄ Kudzu competes with other types of plants and destroys them by preventing the plants from getting sunlight.

▲ Hummingbirds and trumpet vines have a mutually beneficial relationship.

Different species of flowers use a similar approach to ensure their survival. A species of orchid attracts male wasps because its petals give it the look of a female wasp. The wasp carries pollen from one orchid to another of the same species, ensuring pollination. A snapdragon has a flower that will only support the weight of a single bumblebee, which pollinates the plants. And butterfly bushes attract many butterflies that help spread the species through pollination.

A third type of interaction among living organisms is the relationship between a predator and its prey known as **predation**. Hawks, for example, prey on squirrels and chipmunks. Lions prey on antelope and wildebeests. Animals that are likely to be prey for other species use a variety of techniques to avoid being eaten. Rabbits, for example, which are prey for hawks and other animals, generally appear at dusk when they can hide in the shadows.

The monarch butterfly has a poisonous chemical in its body that often prevents predators from attacking it. The viceroy butterfly does not possess this chemical. But it mimics the monarch in appearance as a way of protecting itself. **Mimicry** helps the viceroy escape predators. Through mimicry, it pretends to be a monarch butterfly. Other animals depend on camouflage, like the arctic fox, whose white coat blends in with the snow in winter.

The relationships between various species are part of a process called **coevolution**. Species evolve together in a relationship that may involve competition, mutualism, or predation. The strongest red-winged blackbirds, for example, survive, reproduce, and strengthen the entire species. The strongest lions catch the most prey and reproduce a new generation. Ants and aphids have developed a mutual relationship that ensures the reproduction of both species. Tiny aphids remove the sap from plants. Ants transport the aphids from plant to plant and protect them from predators. Meanwhile, the ants take advantage of the relationship by eating the sap collected by the aphids.

✓ **CHECKPOINT**
Read More About It
Read about the chemicals monarch butterflies use to protect themselves from predators.

Food Chains and Food Webs

Living organisms are linked together in **food chains** and **food webs**. A simple food chain begins with a **producer**. Generally, this is a green plant. Green plants produce their own food. They combine sunlight with water and carbon dioxide to produce sugar. The sugar nourishes the plants and helps them grow. The sugar also provides nourishments for herbivores that eat the green plants. Examples of herbivores are rabbits, squirrels, cows, and horses. The plant and the rabbit form two links in a food chain. The plant is a producer while the rabbit is a **consumer**.

The plant-eating rabbit is a first-level consumer. But the rabbit, in turn, might be eaten by a fox. The fox is known as a second-level consumer. It is a carnivore. The fox might be eaten by a mountain lion, known as a third-level consumer.

The Root of the Meaning
Carnivore, Herbivore

Carnivore comes from the Latin *carnivorus*, meaning "meat-eating." **Herbivore** comes from the Latin *herba* and with the suffix -vore means "plant-eating."

Another link in the food chain is a **decomposer**. Decomposers are organisms like bacteria and fungi. When plants and animals die, they are attacked by decomposers who eat them. Bacteria are found in many different environments. Some bacteria live in the stomachs of sheep and help them digest the plants that they eat. Plants have bacteria attached to their roots. These bacteria help the plants absorb nitrogen, a substance that is essential to the plant's survival.

◀ The green grass, a plant, and the rabbit, an herbivore, form two links in a food chain.

Benefits of Biodiversity

Biodiversity among plants and animals is essential to the future of our planet. The Pacific yew tree, for example, produces paclitaxel, a substance used to fight cancer. What if the yew had become extinct before paclitaxel could have been discovered? Penicillium fungi produce a substance called **penicillin**, used to fight infection. Before its discovery, doctors were frequently unable to save patients who developed serious infections from disease. In addition, penicillin enabled surgeons to successfully treat wounded soldiers in World War II, saving countless lives. Today penicillin is produced in laboratories based on scientists' knowledge of how it is made from fungi. If these fungi had become extinct, penicillin might never have been discovered.

Bacteria in the soil produce another substance called streptomycin. This drug has been very effective in fighting tuberculosis, a disease of the lungs that in the past frequently killed its victims.

In addition to the medical benefits of certain species, biodiversity provides many other products useful to humans. These include wood from trees, used in making paper, building houses, and making furniture. Fruits, vegetables, and nuts are produced by many species of plants. Popular drinks like coffee, tea, and colas also come from plants.

Penicillin, now made in laboratories, was originally derived from fungi. ▼

▲ A fungus is a decomposer that attacks and destroys dead plants.

A **fungus** is another type of decomposer. Examples of fungi are mushrooms and toadstools. Fungi attach themselves to dead plants, such as trees. If you see a fungus growing on the side of a tree, part or all of the tree is probably dead. Without decomposers, dead plants and animals would pile up across the earth.

The relationship between organisms is generally more complex than a simple food chain. For example, a hawk may eat a squirrel that has eaten nuts. That is a food chain. But the hawk may also eat snakes and rabbits. These complex relationships form a food web.

In addition to herbivores and carnivores, some animals are **omnivores**. Omnivores, such as humans, eat food derived from plants as well as from other animals.

Species and Their Delicate Relationships

Various species live in delicate relationships to each other. These relationships are not always appreciated by human beings who may thoughtlessly eliminate a species, upsetting an entire environment. For example, many people believed that alligators in the South were simply a nuisance. They slithered along golf courses, threatening people who played there. Sometimes they attacked defenseless dogs and ate them. As a result, alligators were hunted almost to extinction.

However, as alligators disappeared, fishermen began to notice something unexpected. Fish that they liked to catch were also disappearing. Scientists discovered that alligators ate a big fish known as a gar. With the alligators gone, the gar could gobble up the smaller fish that fishermen liked to catch. As a result, the alligator became protected from hunters in 1967. Their numbers began to increase, as did the various species of fish in rivers and ponds.

Alligators are known as **keystone species**. That is, they play a key role in food webs. This concept was introduced in 1969 by Robert T. Paine, a professor at the University of Washington. Paine had been conducting research on a species of starfish that ate two types of mussels that lived nearby. If the starfish was removed, the population of mussels exploded and drove out many other species.

Alligators play a critical role in the balance of nature. ▶

Another keystone species is the sea otter. These animals almost became extinct in the 1700s and 1800s because they were hunted for their fur. In 1911, they became protected because scientists realized that sea otters played a key role in the environment. They ate sea urchins. Without the otters, the urchin population exploded. Urchins ate kelp, an alga that grows in the ocean. Without the kelp, many fish did not have a place to live and reproduce. Consequently, fishermen discovered that many of the fish they caught to be sold as food were disappearing.

Sometimes human beings make decisions and take actions that have a major impact on biodiversity. Hunting can destroy a species that is critical to the environment. Air and water pollution can also affect important food webs. For example, fertilizers are used on farms to grow healthy crops. But sometimes fields are overfertilized. Plants cannot absorb all of the fertilizer, and some of it is carried off by rainwater into nearby lakes and streams. There the fertilizer nourishes algae in the water, which spread across the surface. Eventually, the entire surface is covered with a carpet of algae, which results in the depletion of oxygen in the water. Fish and other organisms that rely on oxygen to breathe eventually die out.

Fertilizers on lawns can also cause pollution. If lawns are overfertilized, some of the fertilizer runs off into the soil, polluting groundwater beneath the surface.

SCIENCE & TECHNOLOGY

Lawn Fertilizers Impact Rivers and Streams

Many lawn fertilizers have numbers on the side of the bag, such as 10-10-10. This is the percentage of nitrogen, phosphorus, and potassium in the fertilizer. All of these ingredients help the grass grow. But, when the fertilizer is spread on the lawn, some of it may land on the sidewalk or road. Grass containing fertilizer may also fall on the sidewalk during mowing. From there, grass and fertilizer can be washed by rainfall into storm drains leading into rivers and ponds. The result is water pollution.

▲ Lawn fertilizer can cause water pollution.

Summing Up

- Organisms interact with each other in a variety of ways. They compete with each other, prey on each other, and even work together in ways that benefit each other.

- Species known as producers, consumers, and decomposers form intricate food webs. If an important species is removed from the web, the entire system may be destroyed.

- Humans intervene in these food webs and may unintentionally disrupt them. Therefore, it is important that we carefully consider what we do and how it may impact the environment.

Putting It All Together

Choose one of the following research activities. Work independently, in pairs, or in small groups. Share your responses with your class.

1. Research the role of prairie dogs in their environment. Are they a keystone species? Make a food web diagram to illustrate your argument.

2. Prepare an oral or visual presentation on the viceroy butterfly. How does it use mimicry of the monarch butterfly to protect itself?

3. Human beings have an enormous impact on animal species through air and water pollution. Prepare a presentation about the impact of pollution on local animals and plants.

Conclusion

Species

THEIR BIODIVERSITY AND THEIR ADAPTATIONS

Species have developed many different ways to adapt to their habitats. These habitats range from the severe cold of the Arctic, the home of the arctic fox and the ptarmigan, to the extreme heat of the American deserts in the Southwest, the home of the kangaroo rat and the cactus plant. Each environment supports a rich biodiversity of species. Sometimes a habitat changes, and species must adapt or become extinct. Species have developed their adaptations through a process known as evolution, described by Charles Darwin in 1859. Darwin theorized that species that are best adapted will survive and those that are not will disappear. Species have developed over billions of years in the geologic history of Earth. These include a vast biodiversity of reptiles, amphibians, fish, mammals, and insects. These species coexist through various interactions that enable them to survive.

How to Write a Scientific Explanation

WHY DID DINOSAURS BECOME EXTINCT?

Preparation

Scientists pose a question about an event. For example: *Why did dinosaurs become extinct?* Then the scientists try to provide an answer or answers to the question. They assemble evidence to support the answers. The evidence usually comes from several sources to provide adequate support for the answers. The evidence is presented in a clear way so readers can understand it.

Gathering Evidence

Evidence may be gathered from a variety of sources. These sources might include books from the library, websites, and articles from periodicals. Information should include the hypothesis developed by Luis and Walter Alvarez at the University of California about the giant meteor. Other information might include theories that Earth was struck by more than one meteor, leading to an extinction of many organisms. Make sure to evaluate evidence that volcanic eruptions or climate changes may have played a role in the mass extinction. The extinction 65 million years ago might also be compared with the mass extinction at the end of the Permian period.

Writing the Scientific Explanation

- Present the question that you are trying to explain.

- Summarize the answer or answers that you are intending to present in your report.

- Present background information about extinctions in geologic time.

- Introduce the extinction at the end of the Cretaceous period.

- Explain the size of the extinction and what organisms were affected.

- Then focus your explanation on the dinosaurs.

- Present the theory or theories to explain the dinosaur extinction.

- Use as many paragraphs as necessary to present all of the evidence.

▲ Luis and Walter Alvarez developed a theory to explain the extinction of the dinosaurs.

Editing the Scientific Explanation

- Reread your written presentation and check your evidence for accuracy.

- Read through it again to make sure that the ideas flow smoothly.

- Read through it a third time to ensure that the words and sentences are clear.

- Shorten any long sentences, or break them into two sentences to make them easier to follow.

- Check your work for punctuation and grammar.

- Create any visual aids, such as a chart, that may be necessary to reinforce your ideas.

Glossary

adaptation   (a-dap-TAY-shun) *noun* an inheritable physical or behavioral trait that increases an organism's chance of survival by aiding in a species' ability to grow or reproduce (page 6)

amphibian   (am-FIH-bee-un) *noun* an animal that can live in water and on land (page 12)

aquatic   (uh-KWAH-tik) *adjective* of or relating to a water environment (page 7)

biodiversity   (by-oh-dih-VER-sih-tee) *noun* the variety of living organisms (page 9)

carnivore   (KAR-nih-vor) *noun* a flesh-eating organism (page 26)

coevolution   (koh-eh-vuh-LOO-shun) *noun* the change in the genetic composition of one species in response to the genetic change in another (page 36)

consumer   (kun-SOO-mer) *noun* an organism that lives by eating other organisms (page 37)

convergent evolution   (kun-VER-jent eh-vuh-LOO-shun) *noun* when two species develop similar features because they live in similar environments (page 28)

coral reef   (KOR-ul REEF) *noun* an underwater, limestone structure formed from the skeletal remains of a simple type of aquatic animal (page 10)

decomposer   (dee-kum-POH-zer) *noun* an organism that eats dead organisms (page 37)

divergent evolution   (dih-VER-jent eh-vuh-LOO-shun) *noun* when two species evolve from the same ancestor (page 27)

estivation   (es-tih-VAY-shun) *noun* an animal's dormancy during a hot, dry period; the summertime equivalent of hibernation (page 12)

evolution   (eh-vuh-LOO-shun) *noun* process of change or development (page 19)

extinct   (ik-STINGKT) *adjective* when a species dies out (page 13)

food chain   (FOOD CHANE) *noun* a simple series of three or four organisms in which the sun's energy is passed from one to the other (page 37)

food web   (FOOD WEB) *noun* a series of food chains that form complex links between organisms (page 37)

fossil   (FAH-sul) *noun* remains of a dead animal or plant (page 17)

fungus   (FUN-gus) *noun* a type of decomposer (page 38)

habitat   (HA-bih-tat) *noun* the type of environment in which an organism can survive (page 7)

herbivore   (ER-bih-vor) *noun* a plant-eating organism (page 26)

hibernation (hy-ber-NAY-shun) *noun* a period of dormancy during the harsh, cold winter characterized by extreme lowering of bodily functions (page 8)

keystone species (KEE-stone SPEE-sheez) *noun* a species that plays a key role in a food web in its environment (page 39)

mammal (MA-mul) *noun* an animal with hair that nurses its own young with milk from its body (page 29)

mimicry (MIH-mih-kree) *noun* the resemblance of members of one species to those of another species as a means of increasing their chance of survival (page 36)

mutualism (MYOO-chuh-wuh-lih-zum) *noun* a close association between members of different species that serves as a benefit to both parties (page 35)

natural selection (NA-chuh-rul seh-LEK-shun) *noun* process of selecting the strongest member of a species to survive (page 21)

niche (NICH) *noun* the role an organism plays in its environment, or the way in which it meets its requirements to survive in its environment (page 28)

omnivore (AHM-nih-vor) *noun* an organism that eats both plants and animals (page 38)

penicillin (peh-nih-SIH-lin) *noun* an antibiotic obtained from a fungus; used to fight bacterial infections (page 38)

predation (prih-DAY-shun) *noun* when an animal obtains its food by killing another animal (page 36)

producer (pruh-DOO-ser) *noun* an organism that makes its own food (page 37)

salinity (sa-LIH-nih-tee) *noun* the amount of salt a substance contains (page 10)

selective breeding (seh-LEK-tiv BREE-ding) *noun* when breeders choose organisms with specific traits that they want to be inherited by the organisms' offspring (page 21)

species (SPEE-sheez) *noun* organisms with similar features that can reproduce with each other (page 8)

terrestrial (tuh-RES-tree-ul) *adjective* of the land (page 7)

trilobite (TRY-luh-bite) *noun* multicelled organisms that began appearing in oceans about 540 million years ago (page 25)

zooplankton (zoh-uh-PLANK-tun) *noun* microscopic aquatic animals that supply food for larger animals (page 10)

Index